The Suez Canal: The History and Wate....y

By Charles River Editors

A picture of Egyptian vehicles crossing the Suez Canal during the Yom Kippur War

About Charles River Editors

Charles River Editors is a boutique digital publishing company, specializing in bringing history back to life with educational and engaging books on a wide range of topics. Keep up to date with our new and free offerings with this 5 second sign up on our weekly mailing list, and visit Our Kindle Author Page to see other recently published Kindle titles.

We make these books for you and always want to know our readers' opinions, so we encourage you to leave reviews and look forward to publishing new and exciting titles each week.

Introduction

Gregor Rom's picture of ships in the Suez Canal

The Suez Canal

The Suez Canal: The History and Legacy of the World's Most Famous Waterway examines the various attempts to create the canal over thousands of years, and how the modern Suez Canal came to be. Along with pictures and a bibliography, you will learn about the Suez Canal like never before.

An Ancient Idea

"King Darius says: I am a Persian; setting out from Persia I conquered Egypt. I ordered to dig this canal from the river that is called Nile and flows in Egypt, to the sea that begins in Persia. Therefore, when this canal had been dug as I had ordered, ships went from Egypt through this canal to Persia, as I had intended." – Persian Emperor Darius the Great

In 1831, a 26-year old French foreign service official by the name of Ferdinand de Lesseps was sent to Alexandria to serve as vice-consul. While undergoing an obligatory period of quarantine, the French Consul-General, Monsieur Mimaut, sent his new understudy a number of books to help pass the time, and one of these books proved to be a lengthy memorandum composed by French engineer Jacques-Marie le Père, writing on instructions from Napoleon Bonaparte. The subject was the linking of the Red Sea with the Mediterranean by the construction of a canal.

De Lesseps.

Ferdinand de Lesseps

This study made a deep impression on the mind of the young diplomat, and for the remainder of his term of service in Egypt, he applied himself to studying the question. Eventually, he came to believe that it was not only a viable project, but a potentially profitable one too, and, of course, it would be nothing less than a stupendous gift to mankind.

The concept of linking the Red Sea with the Mediterranean was not by any means new. In fact, the idea was as old as trade across the isthmus itself. Work on the Canal of the Pharaohs, or Necho's Canal, as it is more commonly known, began during Egypt's Nineteenth Dynasty, under the reign either of Sethi I, or his son, the great Rameses II. The project sought to link the two oceans through an artificial canal of modest length linking a navigable stretch of the Nile to the Bitter Lakes, and then to the Red Sea.

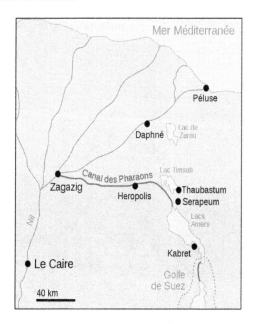

Annie Brocolie's map of the Canal of the Pharaohs

It is not known for certain when or if this project was ever completed, but it attracted the interest of various generations of leadership, and was pushed forward in widely spaced increments over several centuries. It certainly was taken up, for example, and revitalized during the Twenty-Sixth Dynasty, between 610 and 595 BCE, under the reign of the Pharaoh Necho II. Again, during the Twenty-Seventh Dynasty, it was Persian Emperor Darius I who considered it and abandoned it when informed that Egypt lay on a lower level than the Red Sea. Obviously, the belief would be that piercing the isthmus would release the waters of the Red Sea onto Egypt, inundating it entirely.

Under the Ptolemies, work on the project was resumed, this time to be known as the River of

Ptolemy. For a brief period it did indeed succeed in uniting the two seas, but in the end it proved impossible to effectively dredge, and very quickly it was choked up by sand. The Romans, during their occupation, did nothing to advance it although under the Byzantines and the Persians it witnessed a brief rehabilitation as the Canal of the Commander of the Faithful. However, once again it succumbed very quickly to the vicissitudes of siltation, conquest and sand.

In 1798, the legendary French leader Napoleon Bonaparte arrived on the scene. The French occupation of Egypt was, in Napoleon's estimation, first and foremost intended to poke a finger in Britain's eye, and only as a secondary consideration an exercise in the advance of art and science. The two, however, could best be combined in the construction of a navigational canal from the Mediterranean to the Red Sea. The reason for this was simply that the British dominated trade with the East Indies through their control of the Cape of Good Hope. A French-owned canal, however, which the British would be denied access to, would redirect the vast bulk of trade into the Red Sea, through the canal and into the Eastern Mediterranean, granting France effective control of the lucrative Pacific and Indian Ocean trade zones.

Napoleon

In December 1798, Napoleon spent 10 days in Suez, accompanied by several engineers and scientists, including Jacques-Marie le Père, during which time the practicalities of constructing a canal were examined. Jacques le Père was placed in charge of the initial survey, and the results that were returned to him showed that the waters of the Red Sea, at high tide, were nearly 33 feet above those of the Mediterranean at low tide. These results were completely incorrect - there is no appreciable difference between the levels of the two - but that error would take generations to be rectified. The mistake put a damper over any plans to proceed with the project. A complicated system of locks would be required to overcome the difficulty, and that was more than Napoleon was interested in pursuing. The great general eventually turned his mind to other adventures, leaving the scientific and artistic concerns of the expedition to the scientists and the artists. Every detail, including the varying levels of the Mediterranean and the Red Sea, were meticulously recorded in the encyclopedic *Description d'Egypte*, but in the end, Napoleon left Egyptian shores with no serious attempt made to dig the canal.

The next to visit the region and ponder the possibility of a canal across the isthmus was Irish Captain Francis Rawdon Chesney. Chesney was a serving military officer, commander of 7th Company, 4th Battalion Royal Artillery, who was sent to Egypt by the Indian government to survey the isthmus and report back on its potential. This he did, and it was he for the first time since the French survey who suggested that there was no appreciable difference in the level between the two main bodies of water. In general, his report was positive, insofar as he could determine no insurmountable engineering difficulties.

Chesney

However, Captain Chesney discovered what he thought was a much better option, an option that both the British and Indian governments would favor. In fact, they would come to champion it over the idea of a maritime link between the Mediterranean and the Red Sea. This was the Euphrates railway line. The British primarily wanted to shorten the route to India, and Chesney reported, after a lengthy survey, that a better way to achieve this was to run a railway line from southern Turkey down the Euphrates Valley to the Persian Gulf. As far as communication between Britain and India was concerned, this made perfect sense, and it was greeted by the full approval of the British parliamentary select committee formed to look into it.

The concept of a canal was also subject to numerous variations. A canal from Cairo to Suez, for example, was the option favored by the Khedive of Egypt, Muhammad Ali, as well as the British Foreign Office. This would utilize the Nile as a partial route, with an artificial canal linking up with the Gulf of Suez from some point close to Cairo. This project, however, was shelved in the end in favor of a railway line that accomplished the same thing.

Muhammad Ali of Egypt

In the meantime, the young vice-consul already mentioned, Ferdinand de Lesseps, had removed himself from quarantine, and having read exhaustively and studied the ground in detail, he remained convinced that the project was not only technically but economically viable. In 1833, he was introduced to a French social reformer, Barthélemy Enfantin, who was one of the foremost proponents of the Suez Canal project. Monsieur Enfantin arrived in Egypt at the head of a team of some 20 technicians, intending to breathe new life into two projects, the first being the Suez Canal and the second being the Nile barrage. De Lesseps, as Vice-Consul, introduced Enfantin to the Khedive, and while the Nile barrage was approved and construction began on it, the canal was not.

Enfantin

For the next several years, little more was heard about the idea. Egypt at that time was part of the Ottoman Empire, ruled with nominal autonomy by a viceregal khedive. The Sublime Porte was diplomatically under British influence, and bearing in mind that the British at that point could offer no encouragement to anything deemed desirable by the French, the matter was destined to languish.[1] That said, there were some in Britain pushing for the construction of a canal, because it made the most sense of all for British interests. A railway line linking a Mediterranean port with the Persian Gulf would ease the difficulties of communication with India, but it would not provide adequately for the movement of commercial cargo between India and Europe, and certainly not between the emerging British colonies in the Antipodes and markets in Britain and Europe. Neither, for that matter, would a railway link between Suez and Cairo. On top of all that, as commercial steamships grew in tonnage and capacity, the idea of a link from Suez to the Mediterranean via the Nile was also eventually acknowledged as outdated.

Clearly, a canal was the only answer. An uninterrupted flow of shipping from the Red Sea to the Mediterranean would be the answer to every problem, but it would require British rapprochement with the French. Only a few decades removed from the Napoleonic Wars, the British were still unable to fully embrace such a concept. Numerous reasons were advanced for this – for example, Lord Palmerston, British Prime Minister, expressed the concern that trade

---

[1] The *Sublime Porte*, also known as the *Ottoman Porte* or *High Porte* was the central government of the Ottoman Empire.

with the east would be diverted to mainland Europe if Britain lost the advantage it currently enjoyed – and although quite true, none of these concerns were insurmountable. A canal would benefit Britain more than any other nation. The issue was fundamentally political, and not economic, and it dwelt entirely on relations with the French.

Then there was the question of British diplomatic engagement with Turkey. The Ottomans controlled more of North Africa than they did of Asiatic Turkey, and an asset as potentially influential as a canal linking two mighty regions of the world could not be a Turkish asset. That would compromise the British worldview more acutely than a French canal. If a canal came into being, it would obligate the British to seize and annex the Canal Zone, and perhaps all of Egypt. At that moment, the British were unwilling to stir up the international diplomatic hornet's nest that this would entail.

As the British dithered, the French were extremely keen to create such a canal, as was almost every other European power. For that matter, so were the Khedive of Egypt and his Ottoman Turkish overlords. It is proof of how powerful Britain was at that time that despite all of this, and despite the British being deeply unpopular, they were sufficiently feared enough that no one dared to make a substantive move on a project of this nature without the express approval of Whitehall.

Nevertheless, periodic surveys and examinations continued, each building upon the other, and all of them in one way or another concluded that the engineering challenges were easily surmountable. The diplomatic and political challenges were causing the delays, and it would not be until de Lesseps, upon concluding his diplomatic career, embarked full time on the Suez project that the logjam would begin to shift.

Breaking Ground

"The prosperity of the East is now dependent upon the interests of civilization at large, and the best means of contributing to its welfare, as well as to that of humanity, is to break down the barriers which still divide men, races and nations." - Ferdinand de Lesseps

Ferdinand de Lesseps learned the art of diplomacy through the French Foreign Service and honed his skills during a long diplomatic career, much of which had been spent on one mission or another to Ottoman territories. This would prove to be the deciding factor in the eventual achievement of his vision for the Suez Canal. In 1851, at the age of 46, he retired from the service, and thereafter applied himself, from his home in Algiers, to the full-time pursuit of this vision.

At the time, a pro-British Khedive was in power in Egypt, and British interests tended to be pressed in advance of French interests. Then, in 1853, an alliance of Britain, France and Turkey combined to wage war with Russia in the Crimea. The British, of course, were first among equals in this alliance, both in terms of money and manpower, which meant that they held enormous sway in the court of the Ottoman Sultan. What the British wanted, whether it was rational or not, tended to be what transpired.

In 1854, however, Abbas Pasha, the Khedive of Egypt, died, and he was succeeded by his younger brother, Muhammad Said Pasha. This proved to be a watershed moment in the realization of the Suez Canal. It just so happened that Ferdinand de Lesseps had grown up in Egypt at a crucial political moment. His father, Mathieu de Lesseps, served as French political agent in Egypt during the rise of Napoleon, and he was of direct assistance to Muhammed Ali Pasha in establishing himself in the Viceroyalty of Egypt. The younger de Lesseps, therefore, spent a great deal of time as the youthful companion of Said, and the two ultimately became close friends. A bond of family was also established thanks to the diplomatic work of one father on behalf of the other. When Said ascended to power in Egypt, de Lesseps was quick to re-establish contact with him, and to request a congratulatory visit.

Said

Permission was granted, and de Lesseps hurried from Algeria to Egypt. Within a few weeks he had persuaded the new Viceroy to put pen to paper on a concession granting de Lesseps the authority to commence building a canal. A draft was prepared, which the Viceroy signed on November 30, 1854, without so much as reading it, displaying both his faith in de Lesseps and his complete commitment to the project.

This, however, was just the beginning. The concession still required the approval of the Great Powers, and certainly the consent of the Turkish Sultan. The Sultan, however, would not at that point act in a way that was contrary to British interests, so the greater diplomatic contest remained to be fought. It was, however, a start.

The concession, in the meanwhile, provided for the organization of a company that would be constituted as an international enterprise, in respect of the fact that a canal of the sort envisioned could not exist as the asset of a single nation. The Compagnie Universelle du Canal Maritime de Suez, or the Suez Canal Company, was incorporated in Egypt, but it was headquartered in Paris, with 56% of the shares held by French shareholders and 44% by the Viceroy of Egypt, Said Pasha. The Company defined Paris as its administrative headquarters and Egypt as its host country. The key to success would obviously be to frame the enterprise as an international venture, with no single power monopolizing access or control. However, notwithstanding that, the Company was, for all intents and purposes, a French company, based in Paris and with its supreme decision-making elements beign French.

At the same time, the pace of French diplomatic overtures to Egypt quickened. Soon after the formation of the Company, the French Consul-General in Cairo, on behalf of Napoleon III, presented the Viceroy with the insignia of the Legion of Honour, which certainly cleared up any ambiguities as to where the French stood. Napoleon III threw his full weight behind the project, and he would remain a staunch supporter throughout the long diplomatic contest with Britain that would follow.

Napoleon III

Upon the incorporation of the Company and the signing of the Concession, Said Pasha put pen to paper and wrote, as protocol demanded, to inform the Sultan of its existence. In his dispatch, he sought approval not just for the construction of the Suez Canal, but also for the building of a Cairo-Suez railway, proposed and very much favored by the British. Clearly, he hoped that mentioning both at the same time might make the canal more possible. De Lesseps, however, had a considerable rival in Constantinople in the form of seasoned British diplomat Lord Stratford Canning, 1st Viscount Stratford de Redcliffe. A career diplomat of formidable reputation, Lord Stratford de Redcliffe was appointed British Ambassador to Constantinople in 1842, and he would remain in that office until 1858. This term of service covered the period of the Crimean War, and his attitude towards the Sultan during this period lent credence to the notion that Turkey had become a de facto British client.

H. Hering, Photo

Lord Stratford Canning

Victorian author Alexander Kinglake, in his 1863 classic *Invasion of Crimea*, described Lord Stratford de Redcliffe: "He was so gifted by nature that whether men studied his dispatches, or whether they listened to his spoken word, or whether they were only bystanders caught and fascinated by the grace of his presence, they could scarcely help thinking that if the English nation was to be maintained in peace or drawn into war by the will of a single mortal, there was no man who looked so worthy to fix its destiny as Sir Stratford Canning." Lord Canning was also a man of fearsome temper, and with such a passion that what he wished or desired almost always came to pass. Lord Canning, reflecting the view of the British government, was determined to ensure that no canal would be built in Egypt.

When de Lesseps visited Constantinople in February 1855, he found the Grand Vizier enthusiastic about the canal project, but the Grand Vizier was so intimidated by Lord Canning that he would discuss it in nothing but a whisper. As such, de Lesseps was refused any kind of official recognition while in Turkey.

Undeterred after a career of his own in the French diplomatic corps that was no less illustrious than Lord Canning's, de Lesseps was not so easily intimidated. Nominally representing an international company, his efforts were generally effective. The Ottoman administration was supportive of the project, supportive of Said, and unhappy at the degree of British interference in Ottoman imperial affairs. Sensing this, Lord Canning wrote to London expressing an unmistakable note of concern, and he suggested that unless some legitimate objection could be raised by the British government, the Turkish government would inevitably at some point confirm the canal Concession.

That legitimate objection, when it was devised, was both cunning and exploitative. With all of the force of his nature, and with the diplomatic weight of Britain behind him, Lord Canning argued that the cutting of a canal across the Suez isthmus would mark a symbolic and practical severing and separation of Ottoman possessions in Africa and Asia, severing Egypt from Turkey and effectively making it a French protectorate. Let the Sultan forget, Lord Canning shrewdly added that India was originally claimed for Britain by businessmen who acquired minor concessions, and then steadily built up trade privileges in India that were augmented by monopolies and the management of taxation and internal revenues. All of that eventually led to British sovereignty in India. Not so subtly, Lord Canning was implying that the same thing could happen in Egypt. If the Sublime Porte was determined to hand over Egypt to the French, then the British were prepared to wash their hands of the whole matter and leave the Turks to their fate. This, of course, implied a great deal of unspoken diplomatic punishment too, a threat that the Sultan could hardly ignore.

All of this was powerful stuff, and de Lesseps was temporarily checked. He returned to Cairo deeply irritated, but undeterred. Meanwhile, despite British obstruction, support for the project was growing in almost every capital other than London, and Lord Canning realized that without open interference in the decisions of the Sublime Porte, and the open usurpation of the authority of the Sultan, he could not hope to indefinitely postpone the confirmation of the Concession.

At the same time, as far as the French and the British were concerned, a diplomatic truce was declared due to the Crimean War, creating a rather reluctant alliance, and de Lesseps used this opportunity to try and win over the British public. He arrived in London at the end of June 1855 and plunged into a series of meetings and interviews with merchants, financiers, and captains of industry. The official response to this was icy, but his unofficial reception throughout the British Isles was much warmer. The government of Great Britain might have been implacably hostile to the concept of a Suez Canal, but the mercantile, economic, and shipping fraternities were far less hostile.

Perhaps the two major British companies whose influence the government could not ignore were the British East India Company and the Peninsular and Oriental Company, better known as the P&O Shipping Line. The East India Company ran business in India, and a halving of the shipping distance between India and Europe would be of enormous benefit to its bottom line.

On January 5, 1856, the Viceroy of Egypt, Said Pasha, signed a second Act of Concession. To this Act were annexed the Statutes, or Articles of Association of a Company, and these two documents formed the charter of the Suez Canal Company.

Regardless of the ongoing diplomatic deadlock, de Lesseps continued forging ahead, pressing the points of view of private experts and industry leaders over those of governments and parliaments. He returned to Paris from London and convened an International Scientific Commission, comprising eminent engineers from the principal nations of Europe, to finalize the practical engineering approach to building the canal. A final survey was completed in January 1856, and its report was published about a year later.[2] The consensus was overwhelmingly positive, with comments appended to the end of the report mildly criticizing the British government for ignoring all practical, engineering, and economic realities, clinging instead to an outdated view of the project that was driven entirely by political considerations.

British intransigence was brought home even to Britain itself in 1857, when an Indian mutiny required British troops to be rushed to India. With impressive determination, the British transported their forces around the Cape of Good Hope and along the long route. Soon, however, bending to the inevitable military necessities, permission was sought from the Viceroy of Egypt and the Sublime Porte for British troops to be routed via Cairo and Suez, permission which was gleefully granted.

In 1858, two events occurred that somewhat shifted the foundations of British opposition. The Conservative government of Lord Palmerston fell and a brief hiatus ensued, during which the redoubtable Lord Stratford de Redcliffe retired from the diplomatic service. With that, Constantinople was released, at least temporarily, from the tyranny of his influence on the Sublime Porte. At the same time, a highly influential British political figure, the original Liberal, William Gladstone, began exposing the futility of British resistance to the canal project. He argued that control of a facility such as the Suez Canal would naturally fall into the hands of the greatest maritime power on Earth, and if it severed Egypt from Turkey and dismembered the Ottoman Empire as a consequence, then that was a matter of Turkish concern, not a British one. Moreover, he went on, how could Britain stand proud among nations if it was seen to be in opposition to a project that would be of such obvious benefit to mankind? It was, he reminded

---

[2] *International Commission for the piercing of the isthmus of Suez,* or *Commission Internationale pour le percement de l'isthme des Suez*

the British public, a strictly commercial venture, and it should be allowed to stand or fall on its economic merits.

Gladstone

Without the great Lord Canning in Constantinople, the ambassadors of other European countries, France in particular, found themselves in a better position to exert influence. De Lesseps capitalized his company, and he began arguing that the canal was not strictly an engineering project as much as it was the construction of an international highway. Acting on his training as a lawyer, he created a legal smokescreen of definitions and classifications.

Work began in April 1859 at Port Said, but, very little major excavation was done. The construction of infrastructure, in the form of buildings and roads, went ahead instead, while numerous detailed surveys added to the glut of information, and the purchase and assembly of items of specialist equipment like dredgers and excavators were quietly undertaken. Taking note of this, British histrionics in Constantinople reached a fever pitch, and in June 1859, de Lesseps was ordered to suspend operations. He refused to do so, and the Viceroy did nothing to enforce this decree.

Then, Emperor Napoleon III, long a staunch supporter of the project, weighed in, and with the respectful tone of an ostensibly junior partner, put it to the British that de Lesseps and the canal project enjoyed the full and unequivocal support of the French government, and that British resistance was not well thought of in France, or anywhere for that matter. The British were increasingly isolated over the issue. Austria soon pledged its support to the French over the matter, and Russia was quick to follow.

The British shifted tack, abandoning the unreasoned opposition, which had certainly run out of momentum, and instead attempting to seize the moral high ground by voicing opposition to the system of forced, *corvée* labor authorized by the Viceroy. Abolition was a powerful catchphrase at that point in time, with the British leading the anti-slavery movement. Forced labor was slavery, which was the message from Whitehall, and the British stood in absolute opposition to all forms of slavery.

This was a ticklish issue for de Lesseps and his supporters to deal with, and labor contracts were soon introduced, but by then the weight of world opinion was so poised in favor of the canal that work went ahead regardless. On November 18, 1862, the waters of the Mediterranean flowed into Lake Timsah. The first major phase was complete, and by then it was a *fait accompli.*

On March 19, 1866, seven years after work on the construction of the Suez Canal had begun, that the "Definitive Firman of Approval" was issued by the Ottoman Sultan. It read in part, "The realization of the great work destined to give new life and for navigation by the cutting of a Canal between the Mediterranean and the Red Sea being one of the most desirable events in this age of science and of progress, conferences have been had for some time past with the Company which asked authority to execute this work, and they have ended in a manner comfortable as regards the present and the future, with the sacred rights of the Sublime Porte, as well as those of the Egyptian Government…after having read it, we give Our assent to it."

War

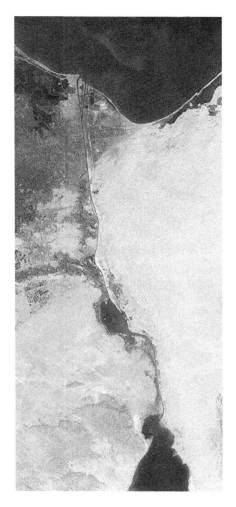

An aerial view of the Suez Canal

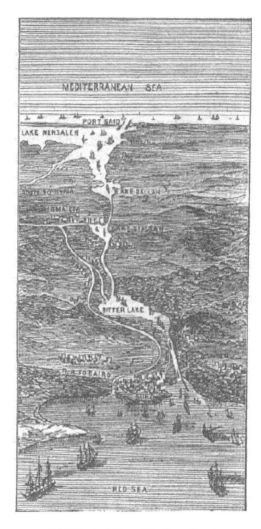

AN 1881 depiction of the Suez Canal

"A beautiful thing is never perfect." –Egyptian Proverb

The Suez Canal was not as great an engineering accomplishment as it was a diplomatic one, but nonetheless, its creation was not lightly undertaken or easily achieved. In fact, its construction was marked as a situation where tools and equipment were invented for the purpose, and generally the question was simply one of scale. Fortuitously, the land in question was comprised almost entirely of sand, and the variations in the elevation between the two bodies of water were so minor that neither locks nor extensive excavations were required. It was, therefore, simply a matter of mobilizing an enormous workforce and introducing dredging machinery on a scale never before seen.

Initially, *corvée* labor was used during the first few years of construction, supplied by the Egyptian government. Following British complaints, contracts were implemented, and pay was on the level of 6 to 8 Ottoman *piastres* a day, more for skilled or European labor. By 1867, towards the end of construction, the standing labor force stood at upwards of 34,000, and 1.5 million workers worked at one time or another on the project. All told, the project took 10 years to complete.

The port of Suez was modified and developed to serve as the southern entrance to the Canal, while the northern entrance was inaugurated as Port Said, in honor of de Lessep's childhood friend. The distance from one end to the other of the Suez Canal is just under 100 miles. A little over 50 miles from Port Said, where excavations began, lies Lake Timsah, a shallow body of water, part of the Bitter Lakes, that carried the Canal a few miles without excavation. Lake Timsah was linked to the Great Bitter Lake, adding another stretch of natural water, before the last 20 miles or so to the Red Sea and the Port of Suez.

The British were furious, but they stuck to the sidelines, attempting only such occasional delaying tactics as sending in armed Bedouins to ferment a labor rebellion. But gradually, as the realization of the project became more inevitable, they began to think more in terms of an ultimate British takeover.

On November 17, 1869, the Suez Canal was officially opened under French control. The ceremony was officiated by Khedive Isma'il Pasha of Egypt and Sudan, and at Isma'il's invitation, French Empress Eugenie, aboard the Imperial yacht *L'Aigle*, was bestowed by the Khedive the Ottoman Order of the Medjidie. He invited her yacht to be the first official vessel to pass through the Canal.

Even at this point, the British were not done meddling. On the evening of the ceremony, the *L'Aigle* was anchored, ready to commence the next morning, with other ships earmarked for the convoy also anchored in their respective positions. A Royal Navy ship, however, the HMS *Newport*, carefully maneuvered itself in complete darkness into position ahead of the *L'Aigle*. Thus, at dawn, to the horror of the French, a Royal Navy ship was the first to set sail down the length of the Canal, followed by *L'Aigle*, which was followed in turn by the P&O liner *Delta*. The captain of the *Newport*, Sir George Strong Nares, was given a severe public reprimand by the Admiralty for the audacity of his actions, but privately he was congratulated, not only for humiliating the French but also for the superb seamanship of sneaking the *Newport* through a mass of ships, in total darkness and without lights, to the mouth of the Canal, entirely undetected.

Nares

In fact, once the furor had died down, the British proved themselves to be magnanimous in . Having stolen the show, they were willing to see the joke in it and let bygones be bygones. De Lesseps was awarded the Grand Cross of the Star of India by Queen Victoria, and he was commended at a banquet held in his honor in London by the Lord Mayor. In proposing a toast to de Lesseps' health, Sir Thomas Dakin remarked, "Our engineers made a mistake – Monsieur de Lesseps was right, the Suez Canal is a living fact." Upon that, de Lesseps was awarded the freedom of the City of London, and presented with a gold medal by the Prince of Wales, who also remarked to the effect that a great service had been bestowed upon mankind.

In fact, the commencement of commercial traffic through the Suez Canal was initially something of a disaster for the British. The British merchant fleet, still largely under sail, could not practically use the Suez Canal simply because of the prevailing west to east winds, so most British commercial traffic from India and the Far East was still routed around the Cape of Good Hope. British competition in international trade suffered accordingly, but once these anomalies had been evened out and the advance of technology gradually phased out the commercial use of sails, the Suez Canal proved to be more of a benefit to British shipping and colonial advancement in Asia and East Africa than for any other nation.

That said, the Suez Canal was still a French asset in all but name, and that would never accord with British foreign policy. The British, therefore, were obligated to find a way of sneaking their frigates to the front of the queue in the world financial markets. That opportunity came in 1875, when the Viceroy of Egypt, Isma'il Pasha, buckling under external debt, sold Egypt's share in the Suez Canal Company to the British for a sum of £4 million. The transaction was initiated by British Prime Minister Benjamin Disraeli, who didn't consult Parliament. That rocked the government briefly, but the deal still gave the British a major interest in the international company.

This began the complicated series of maneuvers that would bring Britain to the point of de facto colonization of Egypt, a status that would carry it through both World War I and World War II in control of the Suez Canal. By then, the Suez Canal had become such a significant strategic asset that campaigns would certainly be contested over it.

It began with the Egyptian Viceroy's plea to the British to aid in a nationalist uprising which gave the British a foot in the door. This period was known euphemistically as the "Veiled Protectorate," simply because it was undeclared, but the British still gained ever-greater control over the Egyptian state. Still diplomatically preeminent in the court of the Ottoman Sultan, British pressure resulted in the 1888 Convention of Constantinople, an agreement that declared the Suez Canal a neutral zone under the protection of the British.

An early 20th century photo of the Suez Canal

As that was taking place, the Suez Canal went into full operation, and once early technical problems and difficulties had been ironed out, it began to occupy a place in global trade and merchant shipping that did justice to all of its early supporters. Decades later, as Europe blundered towards an inevitable war that would be fought on a truly global scale, the military implications of the Suez Canal began to eclipse its commercial application. As Europe separated between the Allies and the Central Powers, Turkey was increasingly wooed by the latter, and it began to seem likely that the Ottomans would enter the war in an alliance with Germany. This inevitably made the Suez Canal a central issue.

When World War I started, one of the first Allied strategic aims was to eradicate the German presence in German South West Africa and to bring under Allied control the ports of that region and various long-range communications facilities. At that early stage in the war, however, the British themselves lacked the manpower and organization to take on this task themselves, and a request was submitted to the government of South Africa, then a newly-minted, self-governing dominion of the British Empire, to undertake the task on behalf of the empire. This was agreed to, and the South African Union Defense Force immediately began preparing for the operation.

At the outbreak of war, the Suez Canal was immediately closed to non-Allied shipping, which created the political anomaly of a facility on Ottoman soil that Turkey and its allies were barred from using. Egypt obviously remained a province of the Ottoman Empire, but practically, it was functioning as a British protectorate. On August 5, 1914, Egypt was declared to be at war with the enemies of Britain, and one of those enemies was Turkey. The Ottoman Army was thought to be massing in Palestine to attack Egypt and regain control of the area, and strong elements within Egypt, most notably the last substantive Viceroy, Abbas Hilmi II, were conspicuously anti-British. Hoping to foment an anti-British movement in the Middle East, jihad was declared from Constantinople. The British responded by ousting Abbas Hilmi and replacing him with his more compliant uncle, Prince Hussein Kamel, entitled the "Sultan" of Egypt.

Upon this, the Turks began to make definitive plans to invade. The first actions were harassing in nature; on November 20, 1914, an Egyptian patrol of the Bikanir Camel Corps was attacked at a point 20 miles east of Qantara by a force of 200 Bedouins. There were other, smaller attacks and raids, culminating in an Ottoman occupation of El Arish, a coastal town just inside Egyptian territory on the frontier of Egypt and Palestine. This was meant to be a prelude to a much more substantial action, and the British moved quickly to bolster the defense of the Suez Canal in anticipation of a major Ottoman offensive.

By January 1915, there were about 70,000 British troops in Egypt, drawn mainly from units of the Indian Army, and 30,000 of these were positioned to defend the Suez Canal. The first serious assault began on February 3, 1915, as massed Turkish troops approached the Suez Canal carrying pontoons and rafts, but they were decimated by entrenched Indian machine guns as they attempted to cross. A bloody day ended with numerous Turkish surrenders, and a clear failure of the anticipated popular rebellion that Turkish and German leaders had assumed would occur at the moment the offensive was launched.

The attack was renewed the following morning, with diversions at Qantara and Ismailia, but British battleships in the Suez Canal and entrenched Allied defenses again drove the Turks back with heavy losses. The final attack faltered early in the afternoon, and Turkish forces withdrew back into the Sinai unmolested by the British. The intention was not to obliterate Ottoman Turkey on this particular battlefield, but simply to announce that the British were there and would stay there.

From then on, nuisance raids by German commanders leading small parties of Turkish or Bedouin troops kept pressure on the British, but no serious follow-up attempt was made by the Ottomans to reverse the British takeover of Egypt. By the end of the war, Egypt was firmly within the British constellation of overseas possessions, and by the dawn of World War II, the Suez Canal, despite still being owned and operated by an Anglo-French consortium, was very much a British strategic asset.

The Turkish raid, while rather limited in size and scope by the standard of the times, inadvertently indicated the extent to which the Suez Canal might serve as a physical, protective barrier against invasion from the east, and vice versa. Its width was on average 600 feet wide, and it was on average 80 feet deep, with the debris of dredging heaped on either side that formed superb defensive shields. Any army attempting to cross would suffer exposure to defensive positions on the far side, and given the nature of warfare in the early 20th century, no military could hope to mount an effective assault without an astronomical loss of life.

An aerial photo of the Suez Canal in the 1930s

World War II witnessed no direct confrontations in the Suez Canal itself, but the contest to control it directly affected how the North Africa Campaign was fought from 1940-1943. The field of action during that campaign covered a region stretching from Northern Kenya, through Somalia, Ethiopia and Sudan, and, of course, Egypt, Libya and Tunisia. Vital to the conduct of this campaign was naval control of the Mediterranean and the Red Sea, which obviously made the Suez Canal vitally important.

Hitler, who was primarily concerned with his conquest of Europe, and later his campaign in the East, was content during the early phases of the war to leave North Africa to the Italians, who were established in Libya, Ethiopia and Somalia. The opening campaign in North Africa was the first substantial Axis invasion into Egypt from Libya, and it was launched by Italian forces in September 1940. The British at that point were extremely vulnerable in the region; their limited Middle East Command had to attempt to secure the entire region with very limited resources. Mussolini saw this as an opportunity to hit the British when they were down and seize the Suez Canal in order to bring about Italian domination of the Eastern Mediterranean and East Africa.

The Italians, however, floundered, and soon after entering Egypt in force under the command of Marshal Rodolfo Graziani, they dug in. Despite various appeals coming from Rome, Graziani could not be moved to advance further. Thanks to the inaction, the Allies were given the opportunity to regroup and rearm, and by the end of 1940, the Italians were under attack and rolling back towards Tripoli on the back of huge material losses. They also lost hundreds of thousands of prisoners to advancing Allied forces.

This forced Hitler to turn his attention to North Africa, realizing that an unsupported Italian Army had no chance of coping with North Africa alone. As a result, the Germans sent the legendary "Desert Fox," Erwin Rommel, who, although under strict orders simply to prevent an Italian collapse in North Africa, took the initiative and sought to seize Egypt and the Suez Canal.

What followed was a see-saw campaign of advance and retreat that saw Axis and Allied armies grappling for control along the vital south coast of the Mediterranean. By then, the Italians had lost Somalia and Ethiopia to a relentless Allied advance, and the Germans were embroiled in what proved to be an unwinnable campaign in Soviet Russia.

At the end of 1942, the United States landed troops ashore in Morocco and Algeria prior to a major advance east against retreating Axis forces. The British, pushing westwards, were resupplied and energized, and the two forces effected a pincer action that trapped the retreating Germans and Italians in northern Tunisia. By February 1943, the Germans and Italians had effectively abandoned North Africa, and soon afterwards the invasion of Italy would commence with the invasion of Sicily.

At no time during this campaign did the Suez Canal cease operations, and at no time did it come under direct threat although on more than one occasion, British control of Egypt itself was perilously threatened.

In the aftermath of the North Africa Campaign, Britain remained firmly in control of Egypt, and Allied dominance of the Mediterranean was absolute. Had the Allies lost Egypt, which certainly was possible on more than one occasion, especially in September 1940 during the first Italian invasion, the course of the war may have been radically changed. Hitler would not have been diverted from bringing the full weight of the Wehrmacht to bear on the Soviets in Eastern Europe, the southern flank of Europe would have been protected, and Allied and British shipping in the Indian Ocean would have been critically constrained. The fight to liberate Europe would have been a great deal bloodier and much more difficult, which at the very least would have meant World War II continued on for much longer.

The Suez Crisis

"Nobody was kept more completely in the dark than the President of the United States." - Anthony Nutting, British Secretary of State for Foreign Affairs.

World War II changed the dynamics of colonization irrevocably. India was granted independence in 1947, and that set the tone for decolonization across the European imperial spectrum.

As it turned out, decolonization was preempted in Egypt by a military coup in 1952. On January 25, 1952, British forces in the Suez Canal region took aggressive action when it ordered a police post in Ismailia to surrender for alleged support of anti-British activities. When the commander of the police post refused and mounted defenses, the British attacked, killing approximately 40 and injuring 70 Egyptian policemen.[3] Outrage spilled out onto the streets in the form of protests and riots, leading to violence, looting, and the burning down of foreign businesses in Cairo.

By July 1952, Colonel Gamal Abdel Nasser's units were moving into Cairo, seizing control of strategic military and government posts and encountering little resistance. One of the revolutionaries, Anwar Sadat, was posted in al-Arish in the Sinai Peninsula when he received an urgent message from Nasser on July 21 telling him to come to Cairo, as the revolution was starting. When Sadat got to Cairo, he found that the revolution indeed had already begun; the rebels had already stormed numerous military bases and arrested top military officers. Following Nasser's orders, Sadat took control of the telephones and served as the communications officer, contacting rebel leaders in the Sinai, the Western Desert, Alexandria, and other major cities in Egypt and coordinating their offensive.

Two days later, on July 23, Sadat was instructed by Nasser to seize control of the Cairo radio station and broadcast an official proclamation to the people announcing the coup. He did, and the reaction on the streets was mixed; though many were overjoyed by the toppling of the British-controlled government and the fall of the foreign powers' puppet, King Farouk, they did not know what was to replace the old system of rule, and whether it would be any different or beneficial to the people of Egypt. As Sadat himself described, there was a "festive silence" in the streets of Egypt's cities that day.[4]

The next job Sadat was tasked with was to communicate to King Farouk the terms of the ultimatum the rebels were presenting – either the king could leave Egypt by six o'clock that evening, or he could suffer the consequences deemed fit by the rebels. Unsurprisingly, King Farouk chose a swift departure; on July 26, 1952, the last king of Egypt left his country for exile in Italy.[5] The revolution that Sadat, Nasser, and their fellow fighters had all dreamed about had finally become a reality.

---

[3] Aburish, *Nasser: The Last Arab*, 35.
[4] Ibid., 33.
[5] Amina Elbendary, "The Long Revolution," *Al-Ahram,* July 18, 2002, http://weekly.ahram.org.eg/2002/595/sc2.htm.

This coup, a minor revolutionary movement, had begun with the limited objective of overthrowing King Farouk, the incumbent ruler, but it became a far larger, anti-West, anti-imperialist and non-aligned nationalist movement. The country fell under the control of an armed forces council known as the Free Officers Movement, and the coup was initially led by Major General Mohammed Naguib, but it would bring about the rise of Nasser.

King Farouk

Naguib

Nasser

On June 18, 1953, the Egyptian monarchy was officially abolished, and the Republic of Egypt declared, with General Naguib as its first president.[6] Ali Maher, who was the former prime minister during Farouk's reign and a veteran politician, was reappointed to his previous position and tasked with forming an all-civilian cabinet. Maher had also served as somewhat of a mentor and advisor to King Farouk, and was well known for his anti-British sentiments. The Free Officers, on the other hand, maintained its position in power as the Revolutionary Command Council, with General Naguib as chairman and Nasser as vice-chairman. Historian Jean Lacouture wrote of Nasser's initial reservations about presenting himself as a leading figure to the Egyptian public that: "[Nasser's] first steps certainly gave no hint that a Bonaparte had come on stage. Nasser was the brains of the movement, but there was no evidence that he planned to take it over." [7]

Nasser tended to be the public face of the Revolution, and it was he who unleashed the most defiant anti-West rhetoric. He also drove renewed Egyptian support for Palestine, in conjunction with a passionately anti-Israeli national agenda. These positions, popular among Arab nations and places still colonized by Britain and France, understandably worried the Western Europeans. The new government of Egypt tore up the Anglo/Egyptian Treaty of 1936, which it was entitled to do, and control over the Suez Canal became a critical issue.[8]

This open Egyptian defiance and hostility towards Britain threatened the general British position in the Middle East. The British were deeply unpopular in the Arab world, mostly due to the role they played in establishing the Jewish state of Israel. During World War I, lavish promises of statehood had been made to the Arabs in exchange for their support against the Ottomans, but once the Ottoman Empire dissolved, the British held Palestine as mandated territory and then handed it over to the United Nations for partition. In addition to making promises to the Arabs, the British also publicly supported the establishment of a Jewish homeland in the region via the Balfour Declaration. At the same time, the Middle East, particularly the eastern Mediterranean and the Levant, were locked in a multifaceted political struggle that presaged the instability of the years to come.

Nasser, who eventually maneuvered himself into power, was leading a nationalist movement that was necessarily anti-imperialist.[9] This, of course, meant being anti-British and anti-French, but the region was also caught up in the struggle for hearts, minds, and resources between the Soviet Union and the West as part of the Cold War. Add to that the emerging crisis with Israel and the Palestinians, and there was a great deal to be wary of in in the region.

Then there was the struggle within the Arab world itself for regional dominance, and Nasser

[6] Ibid., 35-39.

[7] Jean Lacouture, *The Demigods: Charismatic Leadership in the Third World*, 90.

[8] The *Anglo-Egyptian Treaty* of 1936, known officially as *The Treaty of Alliance Between His Majesty, in Respect of the United Kingdom, and His Majesty, the King of Egypt*, was a treaty signed between the United Kingdom and the Kingdom of Egypt. Under its terms, Britain was obligated to withdraw all its troops from Egypt except those necessary to protect the Suez Canal.

[9] Nasser became president of Egypt on 23 June 1956

certainly pictured himself as a pan-Arab nationalist leader, adopting a wider leadership role than the presidency of Egypt. In fact, he considered trading political blows with the British as the opening moves in a wider decolonization of Africa, and no doubt a wider regional role for him. His cause célèbre was the ongoing British and French occupation of the Suez Canal. Some 80,000 foreign troops were stationed along the Suez Canal, holding onto it as if it was sovereign territory. The tensions seemingly made war imminent.

Naturally, Nasser's disdain and distrust of the British and French was wholly reciprocated. The French were fighting insurgencies in Algeria and Morocco, which Nasser was openly supporting, while the British were attempting to adjust to its vastly reduced relevance in the post-war world. Faced with inevitable decolonization, the British government sensed that standing up to a belligerent bully like Nasser would be seen at home as defending Britain's declining international significance.

By 1954, the revolutionary leaders could no longer stall one of the major objectives of the revolution: the complete ouster of British intervention and influence from Egypt. Nasser thus embarked on negotiations for the withdrawal of all British troops. The British submitted their terms, the most notable being that they wished to maintain their hold on the Suez Canal for another 24 months, then retain some of their stores and about 1,200 civilian experts in Egypt for the next seven years. The council agreed, and the draft was accepted. The last British soldier left Egyptian soil on June 19, 1956, and the revolutionary government was finally able to herald the end of the British occupation of Egypt.[10]

The spark that ultimately led to war was an American commitment to fund the construction of a vast dam on the Nile River, the Aswan Dam. This offer was initially made by the U.S. government, through the World Bank, on December 16, 1955. The deal was pictured as an Anglo-American joint venture, but Nasser was at the same time engaged with the Soviet Union to acquire weapons. He recognized Communist China and generally rubbed U.S. and British noses in his increasingly anti-Western positions and rhetoric. The United States, as a consequence, cooled down on the notion of funding the Aswan Dam, and on July 19, 1956, a formal withdrawal of the offer was issued by the American government. The Soviet Union saw its chance to strengthen its ties with Egypt and swiftly offered to finance the High Dam project, further earning the ire of the Western states, but boosting Nasser's confidence and Egypt's morale.

On July 26, 1956, in a historic speech that stunned the world, Nasser announced the nationalization of the Suez Canal. By doing this, Nasser was not only emphasizing Egyptian independence and political might, but also creating another source of tax revenue for the country, which would ultimately be used for the Aswan High Dam project and other social and infrastructure projects. Though many of his advisors expressed their doubts with this abrupt

---

[10] Alagna, *Anwar Sadat,* 44.

maneuver to nationalize one of the most economically significant canals in the world, the Egyptian people were in full support of Nasser, whose popularity skyrocketed as a result.

A picture of Nasser helping to raise a flag near the Suez Canal

The nationalization announcement was greeted with much enthusiasm and emotion by the rest of the Arab world as well. Political scientist Mahmoud Hamad noted that it was only after the Suez Canal's nationalization that Nasser gained popular legitimacy and was firmly placed as the "spokesman for the masses not only in Egypt, but all over the Third World."[11]

Of course, Nasser's sudden move was viewed as an abrupt slap against the countries with vested interests in the Suez Canal and the region at large. In October 1956, Britain, France, and Israel struck Egypt simultaneously – Israel from the ground, and Britain and French from the air – seizing key bases in the Sinai, and in one swift sweep, bombarding all the aircraft that Egypt had bought from the Soviets.[12] Egypt hastily asked for aid from the Soviet Union, which

---

[11] Mahmoud Hamad, "When the Gavel Speaks: Judicial Politics in Modern Egypt (PhD diss., University of Utah, 2008). 96.

[12] Carroll, *Anwar Sadat,* 47.

pointedly refused.

A picture of a damaged oil tanker in the Suez Canal during the fighting

Aid ultimately came not from the Soviet Union, nor from neighboring Arab countries, but from the most unexpected country: the United States. Angered by the fact that the leader of the democratic bloc and Western alliance had not been forewarned about the coming aggression, and deeply affronted by the unilateralism of his European allies, President Dwight D. Eisenhower demanded that the three countries immediately halt their advance and withdraw their troops. In an address to the nation, Eisenhower said, "The United States was not consulted in any way about any phase of these actions. Nor were we informed of them in advance. As it is the manifest right of any of these nations to take such decisions and actions, it is likewise our right, if our judgment dictates, to dissent. We believe these actions to have been taken in error. We do not accept the use of force as a wise and proper instrument for the settlement of international disputes."

Britain, France, and Israel – just as surprised about the forcefulness of the U.S. as Egypt was – had no choice but to comply. Egypt emerged largely unscathed and maintained full control of the Suez Canal, though without the intervention of the U.S., it would have certainly been defeated. As a result of damage and ships sunk under orders from Nasser, the Canal was closed until April 1957, when it was cleared with the assistance of the United Nations. A UN force (UNEF) was established to monitor the Canal Zone and ensure the free navigability of the Canal and peace in the Sinai Peninsula.

On April 8, the Suez Canal was finally reopened, and Nasser's political position was enhanced by the failure of the tripartite invasion, which was largely seen by the world as an attempt to topple Nasser and his government. The crisis gave Nasser instant credibility and earned great popularity and support for Egypt throughout the Arab countries. Leaders of countries across the region sent letters of support and congratulations to Egypt, and "even the Council of the League of Arab States declared the solidarity of Arab governments with Egypt."[13] Egypt was lifted to a leadership role in the politics of the region, as it had accomplished something that no other country in the region had been able to do; it had defied not one Western power, but a coalition of three. The Egyptian victory resulted in Egypt, Syria, Jordan, and Saudi Arabia signing a new treaty, the Arab Solidarity Pact, in 1957, which reaffirmed their commitment to intra-Arab affairs.

One of the Best Anti-Tank Ditches in the World

"The battle will be a general one and our basic objective will be to destroy Israel." –Nasser

After the Suez Crisis, Israel was understandably worried about its security. The nation had come into being through war in 1948, and it seemed that its survival could only be ensured by continuing to be victorious in existential battles. The 1956 Suez Crisis offered Israel the opportunity to seize the Sinai Peninsula, and provide for itself the security buffer that it so badly needed. This security was lost in the subsequent political agreements, but Israel remained alert to any opportunity to retake the Sinai.

Israel was surrounded on all of its land borders by hostile Arab countries, but none were quite as hostile as Egypt. Nasser, emboldened by his spectacular propaganda victory over all of his enemies, was anxious to push the envelope even further. Egypt, along with all of Israel's Arab neighbors, had been brutally drubbed by Israel during the 1948 war, known by the Arabs as al-Nakbah, or the Arab Catastrophe. The war had been started by the Arabs to destroy Israel before it could take root, but in the end, Arab territory was lost, and hundreds of thousands of Arab refugees were driven from their homes.

Arguably the only thing uniting the Arab world was its common desire to see Israel crushed, and it was Nasser who provided the most forceful leadership for this movement. Threats of war and annihilation were a daily fact of life, especially as Nasser consolidated his military cooperation with the Soviets. Soviet financial and military aid flooded into Egypt, and elsewhere in the Middle East. From 1956-1967, an estimated $2 billion in Soviet military aid found its way to the Middle East, including some 1,700 tanks, 2,400 artillery pieces, 500 jet fighters, and thousands of Soviet military advisers, about 43% of which was directed to Egypt.[14]

---

[13] Jankowski, *Nasser's Egypt, Arab Nationalism, and the United Arab Republic*, 83.

[14] Figures provided by the *Britain Israel Communications and Research Center.*

Tensions continued to build. Israeli shipping was prohibited from the Suez Canal, and on May 22, 1967, Nasser blockaded the Straits of Tiran, cutting Israel off from access to the Red Sea. This was, at the very least, a violation of international law, and as far as the Israelis were concerned, it was an overt act of war.

On June 5, 1967, Israeli attacks on Egyptian forces began. The undefended Egyptian air force was wiped out on the ground after a strategically targeted surprise air raid by Israeli forces. The attacks caught the Egyptian forces completely off guard, and Nasser was baffled by why his air force had been undefended and so easily wiped out. He demanded an answer from his commander-in-chief, Field Marshal Amer, who only gave vague answers. Amer then abruptly ordered a full withdrawal of Egyptian troops – an order Nasser's friend and Egypt's vice president Anwar Sadat branded as effectively "an order to commit suicide."[15] A bewildered Nasser demanded to know why Amer did not attempt to establish a defense line in the Sinai and ordered an unplanned full withdrawal instead. Amer simply replied that the line – which was to be ready at all times – had not been ready.[16]

In the days that followed, Israeli troops were easily able to march across the Sinai Peninsula, meeting little resistance from the Egyptians, who were no longer able to mount an effective ground offensive deprived of all air cover. By June 9, most of the towns and cities of the Sinai had been seized by Israeli forces, and on June 10, Israel captured the Golan Heights. A ceasefire was signed on June 11, formally marking the defeat of the Arab collation. As the humiliation of the defeat sunk in, Nasser knew the only option was abdication. However, upon announcing his decision to step down, the Egyptian people called for his continued leadership; as such, Nasser stayed on as president. Field Marshal Amer was promptly placed under house arrest for his ineptitude as commander-in-chief, but he later committed suicide before any trial could be conducted.[17]

The Israelis were then able to turn their attention to Jordan, which attacked Israeli targets from East Jerusalem. This led to Israel seizing East Jerusalem and the West Bank in another quick victory, followed by the Golan Heights, taken with equal élan from the Syrians. Israel now possessed as much strategic depth as was practically feasible, and the fortification of the east bank of the Suez Canal began almost immediately.

Nasser was shocked by this thorough and absolute defeat, the signature moment of Israeli military supremacy. Anwar Sadat would later write in his autobiography that "Nasser's appearance changed drastically. His eyes turned dull. His smile no longer dazzled. His face and hands took on a sickly pallor. Death seemed to be stalking him."[18]

---

[15] George Sullivan, *Sadat: The Man Who Changed Mid-East History* (New York: Walker, 1981), 53.
[16] Carroll, *Anwar Sadat,* 52.
[17] Ibid., 55.
[18] Ibid., 54.

During the three years following the 1967 war, Nasser progressively lost the confidence of the population of Egypt, as well as that of other Arab states. The loss in the war was a blow not only to Nasser and his ego, but also to his idea of pan-Arabism and the strength of Arab unity. The defeat had showed that even when uniting all of their military forces and resources, the Arab countries were unable to resist Israeli expansion into Arab lands, and even lost key areas. The final blow to the Egyptian people, and proof that Nasser was no longer the man he started out as, was when Egypt signed the Rogers Plan in 1969 – a treaty drafted by the U.S. offering a diplomatic settlement to the 1967 war.[19] To much of the Arab population, the treaty was seen as an accommodation to Western powers and an utter refutation of the pan-Arabism ideology, and Nasser's easy acceptance of it was the final nail in the coffin.

The state of the post-war Egyptian economy was also a great problem. Though the war lasted a mere six days, the amount of resources and funds spent to prepare for it took a large financial toll. Moreover, the loss of the Suez Canal and the oil-rich Sinai Peninsula also equated to a massive loss in revenue for the government. Much of the remaining government funds were diverted from the social projects that had become such a cornerstone of Nasser's popular policies to the rebuilding of the Egyptian military and financial support for the Egyptians displaced from their homes as a result of the war. To make matters worse, the industrial sector that Nasser had spent much time and effort into developing began to stall, and by 1970, the Egyptian economy was on the brink of collapse, no longer able to rely solely on internal sources of revenue to sustain itself. [20]

The 1967 defeat thus caused the Egyptian population and much of the Arab world to question the costs and benefits of a pan-Arabist future. Egyptians preferred to retain their position as leaders of a united Arab entity, but they also realized that they did not want this at the expense of Egyptian territory and pride. Nasser lost much of his political capital, and his popularity began to fade, which led to the weakening of popular support for the government. Though the people demonstrated against his abdication immediately after the 1967 defeat, causing him to withdraw his resignation, they were no longer as confident in the leadership Nasser promised. The population now wanted a say in the future of their country, as shown in the mass demonstration of 1968.[21] In response, Nasser announced his creation of what he called the 30 March Manifesto, which called for the drafting of a new constitution that would reform the Arab Socialist Union (ASU), which was the ruling party that had been formed by Nasser. Sadat later called the manifesto "the last comprehensive program given by Nasser to his nation…critical to the country's desperate need for national unity."[22] However, it was too little too late. Demonstrations

[19] Joseph P. Lorenz, *Egypt and the Arabs: foreign policy and the search for national identity* (Colorado: Westview Press, 1990), 34.

[20] Danielson, "Nasser and Pan-Arabism: Explaining Egypt's Rise in Power," 44.

[21] Raymond A. Hinnebusch Jr., *Egyptian politics under Sadat: The post-populist development of an authoritarian-modernizing state* (New York: Cambridge University Press, 1985), 37.

[22] Laurie Brand, *Official Stories: Politics and National Narratives in Egypt and Algeria* (Stanford: Stanford University Press, 2014), 70.

continued, this time calling for Nasser's resignation, and from 1968 to 1970, Nasser's popular support plummeted. There was a strong push by the Egyptian population for radical reforms in the government, and Nasser struggled to deliver.

Meanwhile, a period known as the War of Attrition began, during which a steady, low level of conflict was maintained across the line of the Suez. All the while, Israel worked to fortify its position on the east bank of the Suez Canal, for the purpose, as Defense Minister Moshe Dayan put it, of protecting "one of the best tank ditches in the world." The result of this was the Bar Lev Line, a 93 mile long series of fortifications stretching from the Mediterranean coast to the Gulf of Suez. It comprised a network of trenches, tank traps, observation points and bunkers, and its primary function was to act as a first line of defense against any Egyptian attack targeting Israeli forces in the Sinai.

In September 1970, Nasser died suddenly of a heart attack, and he was succeeded by his deputy, Sadat. Sadat was very much part of the old nationalist brigade, but his interest was less in obliterating Israel than reclaiming Egyptian territory and restoring Egyptian pride. He did not necessarily picture a military victory over Israel as much as an equalization that would lead to a more equitable peace and perhaps swing Egypt away somewhat from its strategic alliance with Moscow. Sadat conceived of a very different war. Israel's mastery of the sky tended to cause the Israelis to rest on their laurels, and traditionally superb Israeli intelligence services were confident that no possible invasion across the Suez could be contemplated without prior knowledge being gained long in advance. Sadat, however, while trying to steer his nation to embrace the West, still had his pick of the Soviet armory. Soviet arms strategy was also evolving, and the development of various classes of Surface to Air Missile, or SAM systems, presented the possibility of throwing an air shield over the Canal Zone while a major armored and infantry assault crossed the Canal and established bridgeheads on the Israeli side. The major risk of an immediate Israeli armored response would be dealt with by various anti-tank, wire-guided missiles developed by the Soviets, and portable for easy infantry deployment.

The plan for the coming conflict, at least from Sadat's perspective, was that once the Egyptian forces were established on the east bank, he would then appeal for an internationally mediated ceasefire which would inevitably require the Israelis to return to the pre-1967 positions. The opportunity also would be made available to the United States to mediate, which would place Egypt within the American sphere of influence.

A military alliance was negotiated between Egypt and Syria to launch a combined attack, with the Syrian government, under Hafez al-Assad, interested not only in regaining control of the Golan Heights but also in seizing as much of Israel as opportunity would allow. Absolute secrecy was maintained, and various subterfuges were deployed to lull the Israelis into believing that a war was not imminent. Indeed, a conspicuous failure of Israeli intelligence to live up to its mandate ensured that this secrecy was maintained to the very last second.

The Yom Kippur War, so named for the decision to surprise the Israelis by attacking on a Jewish holy day, began around 14h00 on October 6, 1973. The Israelis were taken entirely by surprise as a wave of Egyptian strike aircraft crossed the Canal and bombarded Israeli military and air facilities in the Sinai. At the same time, an artillery barrage opened up along the entire length of the Canal, pummeling Israeli positions all along the Bar Lev Line. As this was taking place, a vast Syrian force of armored and mechanized infantry began moving against Israeli positions on the Golan Heights.

As the Israelis struggled to comprehend what was happening and began to mobilize its reserve in the midst of the holiest day of the Jewish calendar, Egyptian troops were moving across the Suez Canal. This was the most daring and expertly executed aspect of the Egyptian campaign. Israeli defenses along the Bar Lev Line were intended as a tripwire, and a point from which a general observation of the Suez Canal could be maintained. The Israelis simply could not contemplate the possibility of an Egyptian operation to cross the Suez Canal, and so the Bar Lev defenses had in recent years been scaled down. Moreover, even if the Egyptians were so foolhardy as to try it, a crossing with sufficient force to threaten Israel would be such a monumental undertaking that it would be decimated before it could begin.

The Egyptians, however, had completed their force build-up in extraordinary secrecy, and they had plans to deal with the most difficult obstacle, the sand revetments thrown up by the dredging operations undertaken during the construction of the Suez Canal. The Israelis had since fortified and augmented these huge embankments, which now stood 60 feet high in places, and to breach them under fire by any conventional means would have been a feat of military engineering beyond Egyptian capability. The Egyptians, however, recalling methods used during the construction of the Aswan Dam, deployed a system of floating high-pressure water pumps. These powered water cannons were in turn used to literally dissolve the high sandbanks in a fraction of the time that it would have taken to transport excavators across the Suez Canal and dig out a breach. As gaps were carved through the sand revetments, pontoon bridges were laid, and within hours trucks and tanks were crossing.

These moves left Israeli troops all along the Bar Lev Line in trouble, and as expected, the Israeli tank division stationed in the Sinai came storming in. As they arrived within a mile or so of the Suez Canal, however, specialist Egyptian infantrymen stepped out of foxholes, aimed their Soviet-supplied missiles, and began taking out Israeli tanks until unsustainable losses forced an Israeli withdrawal. At the same time, a comprehensive air defense umbrella along the entire Canal Zone kept Israeli attack aircraft out of the combat zone.

On the northern front, things were no better for Israel. Syrian forces had captured the Golan Heights, driving Israeli forces back and inflicting heavy punishment on Israeli armor.

For Israel, the situation was critical, and diplomatic telephone traffic between Tel Aviv and Washington reached a fever pitch. As the Israelis scrambled to mobilize their reserves, they pleaded with the United States for munitions and arms. To this day, there remains speculation that the Israelis even considered using nuclear weapons as a last resort.

In the end, once the Egyptians acquired a bridgehead on the Israeli side, Sadat did not proceed immediately with the political side of his plan, which was to appeal for a UN-sponsored ceasefire. Sadat was no doubt impressed by the surprising speed and efficiency with which his army had put the Israelis on the run, and perhaps he contemplated more success.

Either way, a hiatus ensued. The United States and the Soviet Union engaged in a bout of naval posturing in the Mediterranean, and American arms shipments began to arrive in Israel. As they did, and as the Israelis regrouped, the Arab nations dithered over the business of consolidating their unexpected victory. All of this gave the Israelis an opportunity to reorganize, and by October 12, the Israelis were beginning to push back on the Golan.

Soon, the Syrians were under real pressure, and they began to appeal to the Egyptians to launch an offensive in the Sinai to relieve pressure against Syrian positions. Sadat resisted for some time, but on October 14, he gave the order for Egyptian reserve divisions to cross the Suez Canal, and for his armored units to advance deeper into the Sinai. This meant abandoning the cover of an anti-aircraft shield, which in turn offered the Israeli Air Force and revitalized Israeli armored brigades the opportunity to attack and destroy them.

This dramatic reversal of fortunes ensured an ultimate Israeli victory, but it did not resolve the dispute that underpinned the war. The Israelis retrieved the Golan Heights, and they crossed the Suez Canal into Africa to take the war to the Egyptians. This was obviously a deeply provocative move, and it too was intended to place the Israelis in a stronger negotiating position as ceasefire discussions began at the United Nations. The Arab oil embargo, the exchange of superpower threats, and pleas from both the Syrians and Egyptians marked the moment that the war had to end. On October 22, the Israelis formally accepted a ceasefire, and hostilities were scaled down.

A picture of Israeli forces crossing the Suez Canal near the end of the war

Sadat had overplayed his hand, but he achieved what he had sought all along. Negotiations with the Israelis went on for a time and were not concluded until September 1978, with the signing of the Camp David Accords. Negotiated by President Jimmy Carter, Sadat and Israeli Prime Minister Menachem Begin, the countries signed an agreement that called for a formal peace treaty to be signed between Israel and Egypt, diplomatic relations between the two countries, and a withdrawal within three months of Israel from the Sinai. Further commitments were made over the question of West Bank settlements, and a renewed effort to resolve the Palestinian question.

The Suez Canal was reopened to international shipping in 1975, under the terms of a UN-brokered agreement known as the Sinai Interim Agreement. It had been off limits to international shipping since 1967. Before it could be opened however, a major debris and mine clearing operation was conducted, mainly by American and British naval services. The Suez Canal was reopened by Egyptian president Anwar Sadat aboard an Egyptian destroyer, which led the first convoy northbound to Port Said.

Sadat was assassinated in October 1981, and much of the animus generated against him in Arab national and Islamic circles was due to his willingness to accept a separate peace with Israel. However, he achieved his objective of returning all captured territory to Egypt, and he positioned Egypt as an ally of the United States. In this regard, his objectives and strategy in waging war against Israel was successful.

The Suez Canal Today

The Suez Canal has remained under Egyptian management ever since, and its operations have not been interrupted by war. In 1962, Egypt made its final payments for ownership of the Suez Canal to the Universal Suez Ship Canal Company, and thereafter it took full control. The day-to-day operations of the Canal are run by Suez Canal Authority, a state-owned corporation headquartered in Port Said.

In July 1979, the United Nations Emergency Force, formed in 1956 and deployed to the Canal Zone, was withdrawn. There was some effort on all sides to extend its mandate, but this did not occur.

Very few engineering extensions to the Suez Canal have been made since the original work was completed, and aside from minor infrastructural development – such as various bridges, and handful of expansions and developments – it remains at much the same width and depth as originally constructed. It is still not possible for ships to travel in more than one direction, so on a 24 hour rotating basis, convoys are formed either to the north or south, with four bypasses positioned at various points along the way. In 2014, work began on creating a new section that would allow for dual direction navigation of a 50-mile central section.

On a typical day, three convoys transit the Suez Canal, two southbound and one northbound. The passage takes between 11 and 16 hours at a speed of around 8 knots (9 mph). Such low speeds reduce bow waves and wakes, which helps reduce the erosion of the sandbanks.

The Suez Canal is crossed by a road bridge – the Mubarak Peace Bridge, also known as the Egyptian-Japanese Friendship Bridge, Al Salam Bridge, or Al Salam Peace Bridge – a railway bridge, a tunnel and an overhead power crossing.

The Suez Canal functions without locks, simply because of the very limited elevation of the land in between. It also has no surge gates, which means that the ports at both ends and the water currents in between can be subject to tidal events either in the Mediterranean or Red Sea.

According to the Suez Canal Authority, 2017 saw 1,534 ships, ranging from tankers to bulk carriers and passenger vessels, using the Suez Canal. The average cost to tankers or bulk carriers for transit through the Canal is $350,000, which has, in recent years, seen large vessels, in an age of cheap oil, returning to the longer, southern African route.

Nonetheless, in 2014, Egyptian president Abdel Fattah al-Sisi announced an $8 billion dollar expansion program that would introduce the two-way central stretch and significantly increase the traffic capacity of the Canal. The jury is still out as to whether the demand will justify this capacity, and whether high charges will simply drive carriers shipping low-cost fuel and other commodities around the South African Cape.

Online Resources

Other Middle Eastern history titles by Charles River Editors

Other titles about the Suez Canal on Amazon

Further Reading

Britannica (2007) "Suez Canal", in: The new Encyclopædia Britannica, 15th ed., 28, Chicago, Ill. ; London : Encyclopædia Britannica, ISBN 1-59339-292-3

Galil, B.S. and Zenetos, A. (2002). "A sea change: exotics in the eastern Mediterranean Sea", in: Leppäkoski, E., Gollasch, S. and Olenin, S. (eds), Invasive aquatic species of Europe : distribution, impacts, and management, Dordrecht ; Boston : Kluwer Academic, ISBN 1-4020-0837-6, p. 325–336

Garrison, Ervan G. (1999) A history of engineering and technology : artful methods, 2nd ed., Boca Raton, Fla. ; London : CRC Press, ISBN 0-8493-9810-X

Karabell, Zachary (2003) Parting the Desert: The Creation of the Suez Canal, Knopf, ISBN 978-0-375-40883-0

Oster, Uwe (2006) Le fabuleux destin des inventions : le canal de Suez, TV documentary produced by ZDF and directed by Axel Engstfeld (Germany)

Rathbone, William (1882). Great Britain and the Suez Canal. London: Chapman and Hall, Limited.

Sanford, Eva Matthews (1938) The Mediterranean world in ancient times, Ronald series in history, New York : The Ronald Press Company, 618 p.

Pudney, John. Suez; De Lesseps' Canal. New York: Praeger, 1969. Print.

Thomas, Hugh. Suez. [1st U.S ed.]. New York: Harper & Row, 1967. Print.

Arrow, Sir Frederick. "A fortnight in Egypt at the opening of the Suez Canal", London : Smith and Ebbs, 1869.

Free Books by Charles River Editors

We have brand new titles available for free most days of the week. To see which of our titles are currently free, click on this link.

Discounted Books by Charles River Editors

We have titles at a discount price of just 99 cents everyday. To see which of our titles are currently 99 cents, click on this link.

Made in the USA
Coppell, TX
17 January 2023

11245081R00030